U.S. Department of Justice
National Drug Intelligence Center

Northwest
High Intensity Drug
Trafficking Area

Drug Market Analysis

Table of Contents

Executive Summary

The overall drug threat to the Northwest High Intensity Drug Trafficking Area (HIDTA) region in 2010 increased slightly from the threat posed in 2009. The HIDTA region remains a national-level transit, source, and distribution center for illicit drugs, especially cocaine, locally produced marijuana, domestic and imported methamphetamine, and MDMA (3,4-methylenedioxymethamphetamine, also known as ecstasy). More so than in 2009, methamphetamine poses the most serious drug threat to the region. Heroin abuse also poses an increasing risk to the region, especially in some rural areas.

The increasing availability and abuse of high-purity Mexican methamphetamine is the primary drug concern in the Northwest HIDTA region. That concern, reported consistently by officials from agencies throughout the HIDTA region during recent interviews, is also reflected in National Drug Intelligence Center (NDIC) National Drug Threat Survey (NDTS)[a] data compiled in early 2011. Cannabis cultivation in the HIDTA region is also a significant concern, particularly cannabis that is being illegally cultivated under the guise of medical marijuana laws. Additionally, the flow of cocaine transiting the region from the Southwest Border continues to plague the area, driven by increased profits for the drug when it is smuggled to Canada.

Key issues identified in the Northwest HIDTA region include the following:

- Local methamphetamine production has declined dramatically because of ephedrine and pseudoephedrine sales restrictions. As supplies of locally produced methamphetamine have decreased, the availability of methamphetamine from Mexico has increased, sustaining high availability of the drug.

- Late planting and crop concealment practices used by cannabis growers, together with reduced law enforcement resources, have resulted in a sharp decline in outdoor cannabis eradication in the HIDTA region.

- Illegal cannabis cultivation by criminals who are exploiting Washington's medical marijuana law is increasing in the Northwest HIDTA region—some criminals are targeting the homes of medical marijuana patients and caregivers to steal high-potency medical marijuana.

- Heroin abuse is increasing in the Northwest HIDTA region, fueled by high availability and an increasing number of prescription opioid abusers who are switching to heroin because the drug is cheaper and easier to obtain.

---

a. The NDTS is conducted annually by NDIC to solicit information from a representative sample of state and local law enforcement agencies. NDIC uses this information to produce national, regional, and state estimates of various aspects of drug trafficking activities. NDTS data reflect agencies' perceptions based on their analysis of criminal activities that occurred within their jurisdictions during the past year. NDTS 2011 data cited in this report are raw, unweighted responses from federal, state, and local law enforcement agencies solicited through either NDIC or the Office of National Drug Control Policy (ONDCP) HIDTA program as of February 16, 2011.

- The flow of cocaine from the Northwest HIDTA region into Canada is increasing because of significant profit potential associated with cocaine distribution in Canada.

Key Issues[b]

Local methamphetamine production has declined dramatically because of ephedrine and pseudoephedrine sales restrictions. As supplies of locally produced methamphetamine have decreased, the availability of methamphetamine from Mexico has increased, sustaining high availability of the drug.

National and state laws that restrict ephedrine and pseudoephedrine sales[c] have reduced local methamphetamine production significantly, evidenced by far fewer laboratory seizures than in previous years. The number of methamphetamine laboratories seized in the Northwest HIDTA region decreased 92 percent from 2005 (181 laboratories) through 2010 (14 laboratories).[1] (See Table 1 on page 3.) Methamphetamine production in the region is typically limited to small laboratories capable of producing fewer than 2 ounces of methamphetamine per production cycle.[2] These small-capacity laboratories are operated by individuals who are able, to some small extent, to circumvent ephedrine and pseudoephedrine sales restrictions. These individuals usually engage in smurfing[d] operations to acquire the necessary precursor chemicals to produce methamphetamine.[3]

Despite the decrease in local methamphetamine production, drug availability data and law enforcement reporting indicate high and increasing methamphetamine availability because of an increased supply of methamphetamine from Mexico.[4] In fact, according to law enforcement officials, most of the methamphetamine available in the HIDTA region is Mexican methamphetamine.[5] Moreover, most law enforcement agency respondents to the 2011 NDTS (23 of 39) in the Northwest HIDTA region report that methamphetamine availability is high in their areas. Supporting the assertions of law enforcement officials are methamphetamine seizure and price data that indicate increasing availability of the drug. For example, according to Northwest HIDTA officials, the number of methamphetamine seizure incidents increased from 151 in 2009 to 249 in 2010,[e] indicating increased methamphetamine availability.[6] Further, the total amount of methamphetamine seized through HIDTA initiatives increased 114 percent from 2009 (119 kg) to 2010 (255 kg). In fact, the amount of methamphetamine seized in 2010 was the highest in the region since 2005. (See Table 2 on page 3.) Wholesale and retail prices for Mexican methamphetamine have declined in some drug markets, such as Spokane, Tacoma, and Yakima, indicating greater availability of the drug.[7] In Spokane, for example, the price of methamphetamine decreased significantly from a range of $16,000 to $23,000 per pound in 2009 to a range of $12,000 to $16,000 per pound in 2010, and the price for an ounce of methamphetamine decreased from a range of $1,000 to $1,800 in 2009 to a range of $1,000 to $1,200 in 2010.[8]

---

b. For a general overview of the drug threat in the Northwest HIDTA region, please see Appendix A.

c. The federal Combat Methamphetamine Epidemic Act (CMEA) of 2005 requires all states to have regulated sellers maintain logbooks and set time-sensitive quantity limits on products containing ephedrine, pseudoephedrine, or phenylpropanolamine. The Revised Code of Washington (RCW) 69.43 of 2005 mandates point-of-sale restrictions on ephedrine and pseudoephedrine products and requires an electronic sales tracking system for those products.

d. Smurfing is a method used by some methamphetamine and precursor chemical traffickers to acquire large quantities of pseudoephedrine. Individuals purchase pseudoephedrine in quantities at or below legal thresholds from multiple retail locations. Traffickers often enlist the assistance of several associates in smurfing operations to increase the speed with which chemicals are acquired.

e. Northwest HIDTA statistics for methamphetamine include all types of methamphetamine.

Table 1. Methamphetamine Laboratory Seizures, Northwest HIDTA Counties and the State of Washington, 2005–2010

County	2005	2006	2007	2008	2009	2010
Benton	6	1	0	0	2	0
Clark	3	3	1	1	0	0
Cowlitz	1	3	3	2	0	0
Franklin	2	0	0	0	0	0
King	32	6	5	2	0	0
Kitsap	6	1	2	7	1	2
Lewis	2	4	0	1	0	0
Pierce	82	32	36	14	7	9
Skagit	3	2	1	0	1	0
Snohomish	27	6	3	0	2	1
Spokane	6	4	3	2	3	2
Thurston	8	0	1	0	2	0
Whatcom	2	3	0	0	0	0
Yakima	1	3	1	0	0	0
HIDTA Total	**181**	**68**	**56**	**29**	**18**	**14**
State Total	**211**	**81**	**61**	**30**	**20**	**15**

Source: National Seizure System.

Table 2. Drugs Seized During Northwest HIDTA Initiatives, in Kilograms, 2005–2010

Drug	2005	2006	2007	2008	2009	2010	Totals
Cocaine/Crack Cocaine	646	937	1,211	2,027	1,388	974	**7,183**
Heroin	14	26	54	14	48	122	**278**
Marijuana	11,397	7,617	6,019	10,433	4,049	558	**40,073**
Methamphetamine	83	100	111	175	119	255	**843**
Prescription Drugs*	8,069	11,962	3,209	6,076	6,070	9,143	**44,529**

Source: Northwest High Intensity Drug Trafficking Area.
*In dosage units.

Figure 1. Outdoor Cannabis Eradication, Washington, 2010

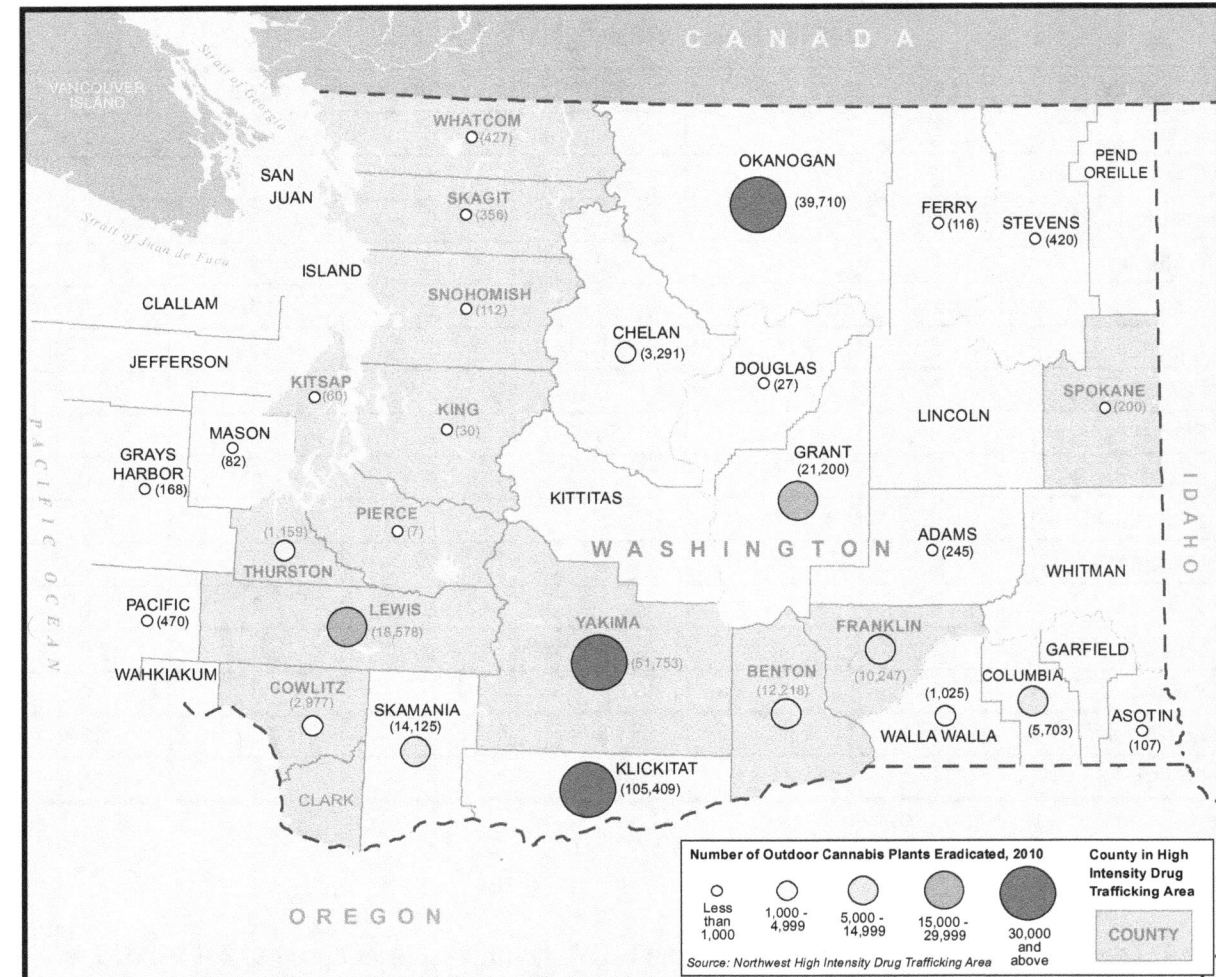

Late planting and crop concealment practices used by cannabis growers, together with reduced law enforcement resources, have resulted in a sharp decline in outdoor cannabis eradication in the HIDTA region.

The amount of outdoor cannabis eradicated in the Northwest HIDTA region decreased sharply in 2010 as a number of factors limited the ability of law enforcement officials to detect illicit cannabis crops.[9] Unusually cold weather conditions during May delayed outdoor cannabis planting for many growers, resulting in smaller plants that were more difficult to detect during eradication operations.[10] Cultivators also adapted to law enforcement aerial detection by planting numerous smaller, more isolated grow sites rather than large single plots.[11] Further, funding for cannabis eradication was reduced, limiting law enforcement air detection and ground eradication operations.[12] The cumulative effect of these factors resulted in the number of outdoor plants eradicated in the HIDTA region decreasing 39 percent from 2009 (171,257 plants) to 2010 (103,675 plants), with most eradication occurring in remote, rural locations. (See Figure 1.)

The eradication of indoor cannabis plants within HIDTA counties increased slightly in 2010, possibly because of increased illegal medical marijuana cultivation within the region (see discussion on page 5).

Figure 2. Indoor Cannabis Eradication, Washington, 2010

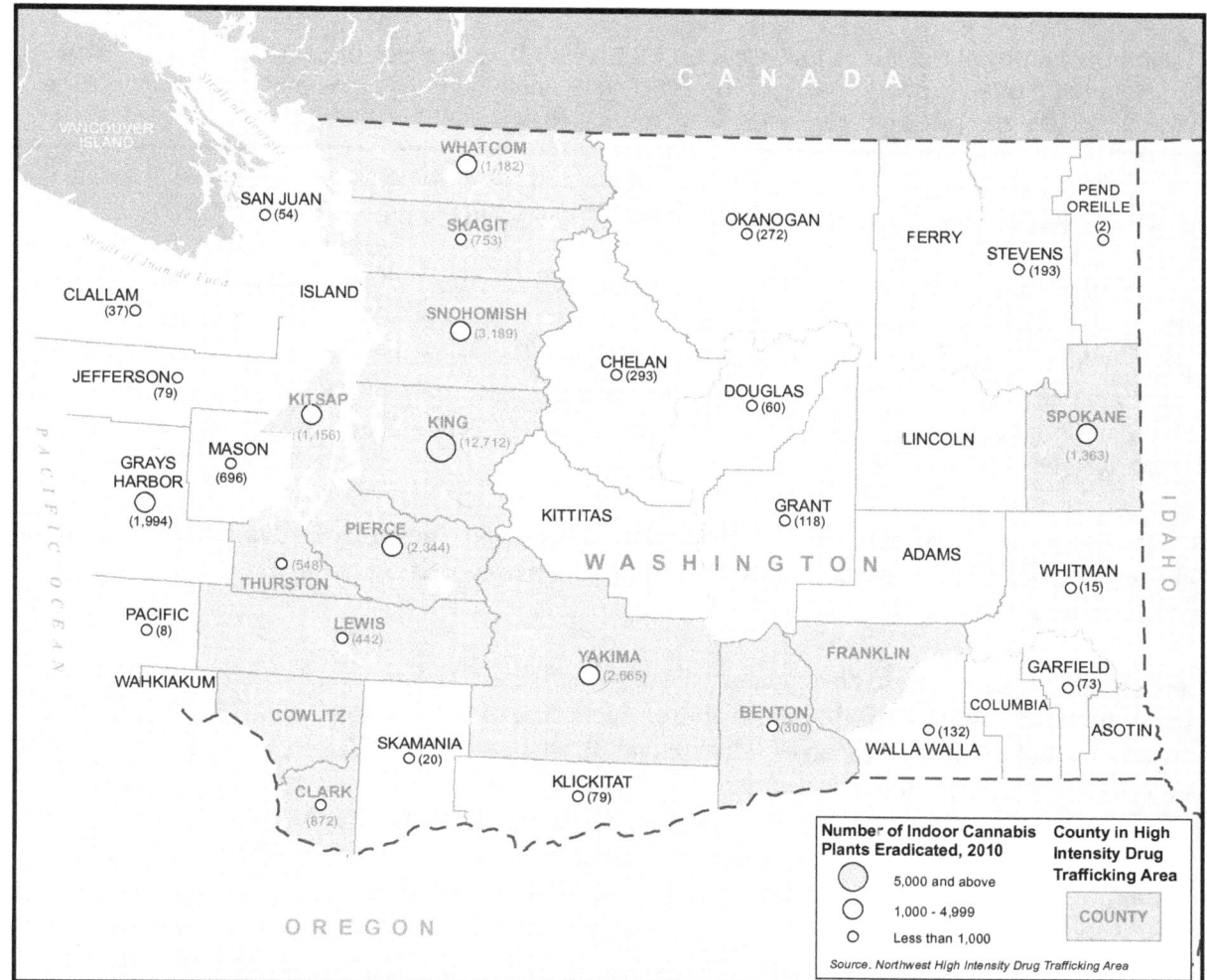

The number of indoor cannabis plants seized in HIDTA counties increased 5.5 percent from 2009 (28,721) to 2010 (30,303). (See Figure 2.)

Although eradication decreased sharply overall, Washington remained among the leading cannabis cultivation states in 2010, ranking fifth in the nation in the number of outdoor cannabis plants eradicated.[13] The large amount of cannabis that is cultivated in Washington and never detected or eradicated supplies local drug markets and those in Illinois, New York, and Pennsylvania.[14]

Illegal cannabis cultivation by criminals who are exploiting Washington's medical marijuana law is increasing in the Northwest HIDTA region—some criminals are targeting the homes of medical marijuana patients and caregivers to steal high-potency medical marijuana.

Law enforcement officials report that indoor medical marijuana cultivation is increasing in Northwest HIDTA counties.[15] Some cultivators are illegally cultivating cannabis under the umbrella of Washington's medical marijuana law (see text box on page 6), producing quantities of marijuana in excess of prescribed limits and selling the excess to abusers in the region.[16] Such activity is especially prevalent in

Washington's Medical Marijuana Law
Washington's medical marijuana law (Chapter 69.51A RCW) authorizes patients and their primary caregivers (who often grow cannabis on behalf of their patients) to possess a 60-day supply of the drug, defined as up to 24 ounces of marijuana and up to 15 cannabis plants under cultivation.

Yakima County, according to Northwest HIDTA officials.[17] Law enforcement officials also indicate that they often encounter weapons at medical marijuana grow sites in the region.[18]

Some criminals are increasingly targeting individuals who they believe possess medical marijuana or who are cultivating cannabis plants on behalf of patients.[19] For example, in March 2010, a medical marijuana patient residing in Orting (Pierce County) was killed by criminals who were attempting to steal his cannabis plants.[20] During that same month, a home invasion robbery occurred at the home of a medical marijuana grower and activist in Kirkland (King County), resulting in an exchange of gunfire between the homeowner and the criminals.[21]

Heroin abuse is increasing in the Northwest HIDTA region, fueled by high availability and an increasing number of prescription opioid abusers who are switching to heroin use because the drug is cheaper and easier to obtain.

Heroin availability and abuse have increased sharply in the HIDTA region, as indicated by a rising number of treatment admissions for heroin abuse. According to the Washington State Department of Social and Health Services, Division of Alcohol and Substance Abuse (DASA), the number of admissions for heroin at publicly funded treatment centers in HIDTA counties increased 28 percent from 2008 (3,268 admissions) to 2009 (4,170 admissions). The highest number of heroin-related treatment admissions (1,592) occurred in King County, which encompasses the metropolitan area of Seattle, accounting for 38 percent of all such admissions in the HIDTA region in 2009. Although treatment admissions for heroin increased in almost every county (admissions in Yakima County decreased by 2) from 2008 to 2009, the most significant increases occurred outside the Seattle area, often in more rural counties. To exemplify, heroin treatment admissions in King County (Seattle) increased only 21 percent (1,312 to 1,592) from 2008 to 2009, compared with a 32 percent (1,956 to 2,578) overall increase in the other HIDTA counties during the same period. (See Table 3 on page 7.)

The increase in heroin abuse is supported by increasing heroin availability. According to 2011 NDTS data, 36 of 39 agency respondents reported high or moderate heroin availability in their areas, a much higher number than for any other drug excluding marijuana. Drug seizure and price data further indicate that the already high level of heroin availability is increasing. The amount of heroin seized in the Northwest HIDTA region increased 154 percent from 2009 (48 kg) to 2010 (122 kg). (See Table 2 on page 3.) Similarly, the number of heroin seizure incidents increased from 79 to 179 during the same period.[22] Further, retail prices for heroin have declined in some drug markets. For example, the retail price for heroin decreased in Seattle from a range of $200 to $500 per ounce in 2009 to a range of $200 to $450 per ounce in 2010. Likewise, the retail price for heroin in Spokane decreased from a range of $450 to $1,200 per ounce in 2009 to a range of $400 to $500 per ounce in 2010.[23]

With the increasing availability of heroin in the HIDTA region, law enforcement officials and drug treatment providers report that some prescription opioid abusers are switching to heroin because it

Table 3. Heroin Public Treatment Center Admissions, Northwest HIDTA Counties, 2004–2009*

HIDTA County	2004	2005	2006	2007	2008	2009
Benton	28	21	19	29	18	33
Clark	101	244	204	192	233	270
Cowlitz	93	97	82	117	157	194
Franklin	10	5	6	3	4	11
King	989	1,850	1,491	1,177	1,312	1,592
Kitsap	46	35	48	41	62	72
Lewis	28	39	22	16	26	34
Pierce	267	267	388	368	281	358
Skagit	152	141	148	137	157	241
Snohomish	288	315	339	261	272	357
Spokane	178	148	173	229	271	405
Thurston	80	125	73	86	114	159
Whatcom	94	144	153	156	207	292
Yakima	138	123	156	161	154	152
HIDTA Total	**2,492**	**3,554**	**3,302**	**2,973**	**3,268**	**4,170**
State Total	**2,662**	**3,739**	**3,498**	**3,182**	**3,493**	**4,474**

Source: Washington State Department of Social and Health Services, Division of Alcohol and Substance Abuse.
*Table is based on Washington's state fiscal year, which runs from July through June.

is often less expensive and more available than prescription opioids.[24] Many oxycodone abusers, for example, ingest 400 milligrams of the drug per day (five 80-milligram tablets), costing approximately $400.[25] Alternatively, oxycodone abusers who switch to heroin could purchase 2 grams of Mexican black tar heroin (the most common type available) to support a single day of use for approximately $20 to $30 in the Seattle area.[26]

The flow of cocaine from the Northwest HIDTA region into Canada is increasing because of significant profit potential associated with cocaine distribution in Canada.

Cocaine is most often smuggled into Canada from the Northwest HIDTA region, and drug seizure data indicate a sharp increase in the amount of cocaine transiting the HIDTA region en route to Canada.[27] According to the Pacific Integrated Border Intelligence Team (IBIT),[f] the amount of northbound cocaine seized at or near the U.S.–Canada border[g] increased 68 percent from 2009 (932 kg) to 2010 (1,565 kg).[28] In fact, in 2010, approximately 21 percent[h] of all cocaine seizures reported to the Northwest HIDTA was destined for Canada.[29]

---

f.　The Pacific IBIT reports for the states of Idaho, Montana, and Washington.

g.　The IBIT seizure statistics include 311 kilograms of cocaine that transited through the IBIT area of operations but was interdicted away from the border in 2009 and 1,001 kilograms of cocaine that transited through the IBIT area of operations but was interdicted away from the border in 2010.

h.　Eleven out of 53 total cocaine seizures reported to the Northwest HIDTA in 2010 were destined for Canada. The Northwest HIDTA receives information on drug seizures that occur in the state or in other states that have a nexus to Washington.

Increased cocaine smuggling from the Northwest HIDTA region into Canada is occurring because of a higher price for cocaine in Canada that affords smugglers[i] an opportunity to gain substantial profit for each successful delivery or trade for other drugs (see textbox.) For example, cocaine purchased in Seattle for $18,500 to $25,000 per kilogram can be sold in Vancouver for $35,000 to $40,000 per kilogram.[30]

Trading Cocaine for Canadian Marijuana and MDMA

Cocaine smuggled through the HIDTA region into Canada is sometimes exchanged for high-potency Canadian marijuana and MDMA, which are then smuggled back into the region.[31] Criminal groups, such as mixed Asian and East Indian, El Salvadoran, and Honduran drug trafficking organizations (DTOs)[32] and the Hells Angels Motorcycle Club, commonly smuggle cocaine through Washington into Canada, but Mexican traffickers have begun smuggling cocaine into Canada as well, according to the Pacific IBIT.[33] When trading cocaine for Canadian marijuana and MDMA in Canada, these groups often use exchange rates that result in substantially increased profits for them when the drugs are smuggled into the United States.[34]

Outlook

NDIC assesses with high confidence[j] that the influence of Mexican criminal groups distributing methamphetamine will increase as they displace local methamphetamine producers and become the only reliable source for the drug in the region. NDIC also assesses with high confidence that demand for methamphetamine will stabilize with sufficient availability to supply current and new users.

NDIC assesses with high confidence that the demand for heroin will increase in the near term as more prescription opioid abusers switch to cheaper and more available heroin—a heroin user in the region would typically need to spend only a fraction of what a comparable prescription opioid addiction would cost to maintain.

---

i. Various transporter groups smuggle cocaine both through and between the ports of entry (POEs) along the U.S.–Canada border. These groups are typically several levels removed from the organized crime groups they work for and are usually not directly affiliated with any one organized crime group.

j. **High Confidence** generally indicates that the judgments are based on high-quality information or that the nature of the issue makes it possible to render a solid judgment. **Medium Confidence** generally means that the information is credibly sourced and plausible but can be interpreted in various ways, or is not of sufficient quality or corroborated sufficiently to warrant a higher level of confidence. **Low Confidence** generally means that the information is too fragmented or poorly corroborated to make a solid analytic inference, or that there are significant concerns or problems with the sources.

Appendix A. Northwest HIDTA Overview

Map A1. Northwest High Intensity Drug Trafficking Area

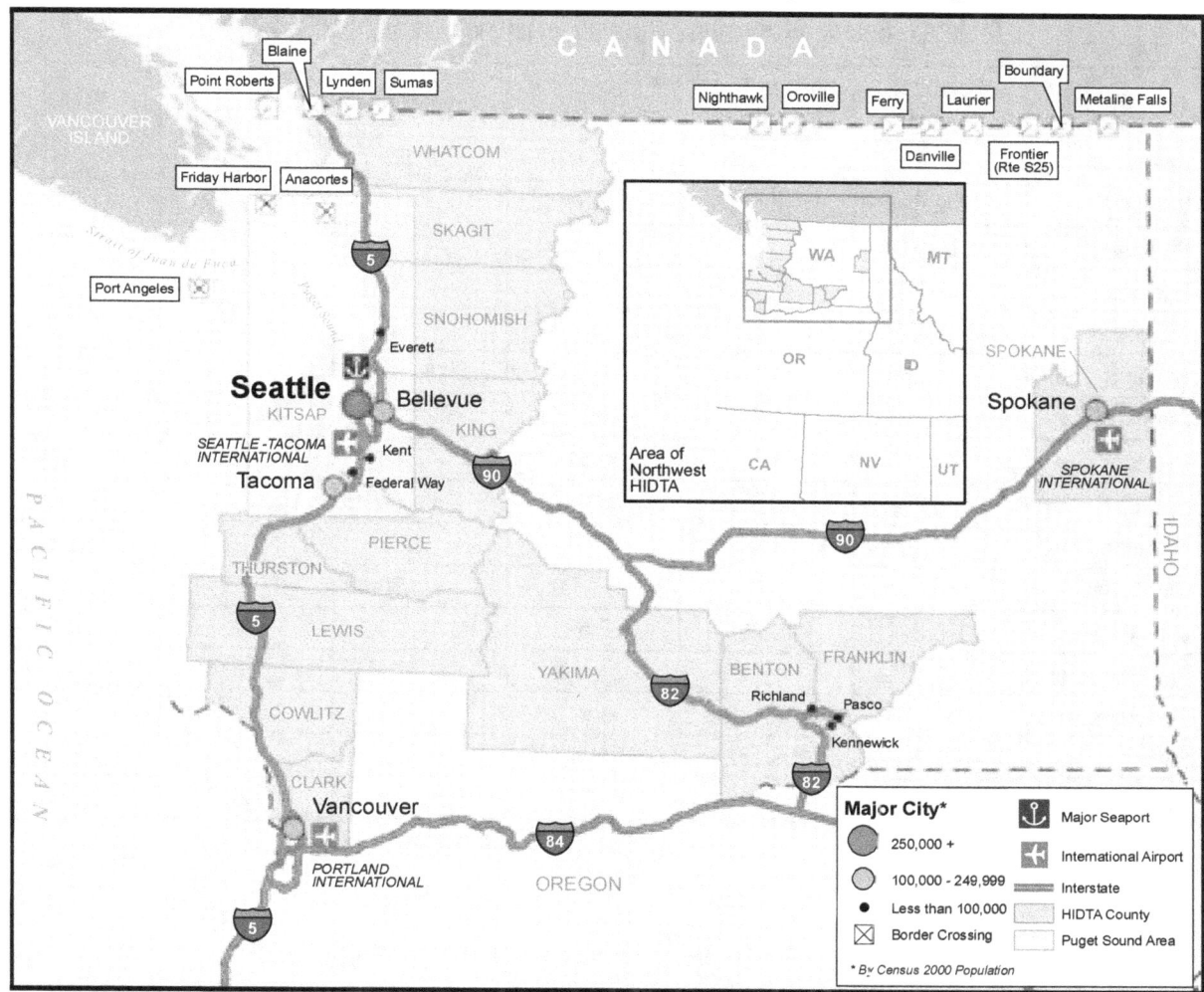

The Northwest HIDTA region encompasses 14 counties in Washington—Benton, Clark, Cowlitz, Franklin, King, Kitsap, Lewis, Pierce, Skagit, Snohomish, Spokane, Thurston, Whatcom, and Yakima. (See Map A1.) Almost 29 percent of the entire population of the state resides in King County, the most populous county in the state, which encompasses Seattle.[35] The proximity of the Northwest HIDTA region to Canada and direct access to drug sources in Mexico through a vast transportation infrastructure—numerous freeways, highways, airports, waterways, and railways—contribute to the threat of cross-border smuggling. Many areas along the Olympic Peninsula are very remote, and the geography makes it difficult for any single law enforcement agency to deal with the ongoing threat of narcotics smuggling and distribution, which is why the U.S. Customs and Border Protection (CBP) maritime interdiction unit works closely with the U.S. Coast Guard in the region.[36] The high volume of traffic at the 15 land ports of entry (POEs) along these borders and the remote, relatively porous areas between POEs are routinely exploited by traffickers smuggling illicit drugs to the region. Blaine (WA) is the busiest land POE in the Pacific Region for all types of vehicular and pedestrian traffic; in 2009, more than 3 million private vehicles and trucks entered Washington from

Canada at the Blaine POE. (See Table A1.) Interstate 5, a major north-south corridor, also provides traffickers direct access to the area from the San Ysidro and Otay Mesa POEs at the U.S.–Mexico border and the Blaine POE located in Washington at the U.S.–Canada border.

Table A1. Inbound Crossings Through Washington Land POEs, 2009*

POE	Personal Vehicles	Loaded Truck Containers	Empty Truck Containers	Pedestrians	Buses	Trains
Anacortes	27,137	0	0	14,412	12	0
Blaine	2,842,631	217,622	93,340	0	15,159	1,349
Boundary	65,218	24	14	156	21	250
Danville	50,848	0	0	528	0	0
Ferry	8,972	0	0	181	14	0
Friday Harbor	2,356	0	0	3,557	1	0
Frontier	37,798	11,201	7,917	112	98	0
Laurier	46,191	1,605	514	86	35	83
Lynden	546,850	18,070	25,627	2,154	9	0
Metaline Falls	24,109	1,407	3,417	134	69	0
Nighthawk	10,110	0	0	36	0	0
Oroville	328,342	19,265	9,558	726	233	0
Point Roberts	722,725	0	0	11,648	815	0
Port Angeles	57,232	0	0	0	83	0
Sumas	672,262	106,962	21,564	27,022	1,128	238
Total	**5,442,781**	**376,156**	**161,951**	**60,752**	**17,677**	**1,920**

Source: U.S. Department of Transportation.

*The latest year for which such data are available.

Mexican DTOs and criminal groups are the principal wholesale distributors of methamphetamine, cocaine, and heroin, which they transport into the Northwest HIDTA region using the Interstate 5 corridor.[37] The primary destination for most of these drugs is the Seattle metropolitan area, which includes the cities of Seattle, Tacoma, and Everett.[38]

Marijuana is also a readily available and frequently abused drug in the Northwest HIDTA region; 37 of the 39 state and local law enforcement respondents to the NDTS 2011 report that the drug is highly available throughout the area. Mexican DTOs and criminal groups operate most of the large outdoor cannabis grow operations in the region and are known to cultivate cannabis on tribal lands, such as the Yakima Indian Reservation in Yakima County, sometimes working with local Native Americans.[39] For example, in 2010, 117,295 cannabis plants were eradicated from U.S. Forest Service lands and 81,874 cannabis plants were eradicated from Bureau of Indian Affairs/tribal lands in Washington.[40] Cannabis grown under the auspices of the medical marijuana law, often cultivated indoors, is prevalent throughout the region, and many cultivators continue to grow plants in excess of the legal amount prescribed by the state.[41] Asian DTOs (primarily Vietnamese) and outlaw motorcycle gangs (OMGs), particularly Hells Angels, also smuggle significant quantities of Canada-produced marijuana and MDMA into the region and traffic cocaine through the region into Canada.[42]

Heroin and controlled prescription drugs (CPDs), especially prescription opioids, are increasing drug threats in the Northwest HIDTA region.[43] Increasing amounts of heroin are being smuggled into the area by Mexican DTOs, and seizures of the drug continue to increase.[44] Treatment professionals report that some prescription opioid abusers are switching to heroin when it becomes less costly or more available than the prescription opioids they abuse.[45]

Cocaine is readily available in the Northwest HIDTA region as it is smuggled through the region into Canada for consumption.[46] Traffickers routinely take advantage of the direct route from the Southwest Border to Canada running through the region along Interstate 5.[47]

The distribution and abuse of MDMA are major concerns to law enforcement in the Northwest HIDTA region. Much of the MDMA manufactured in Canada and destined for U.S. markets transits the region and, as such, poses a significant risk, particularly in market areas such as Seattle, where a large college-age population creates increased demand for the drug.[48] Canada-based Chinese and Vietnamese MDMA producers often add caffeine, ephedrine, ketamine, and methamphetamine, among other substances, to MDMA as cheap filler ingredients to increase their profits or to stretch their supplies of MDMA.[49] Moreover, BZP (N-benzylpiperazine) tablets produced in Canada are sometimes sold as MDMA to unsuspecting abusers or, on occasion, as an alternative to MDMA.[50] However, in the Pacific IBIT area of operation in 2010, there were no recorded seizures of BZP coming from Canada. This may indicate that BZP, considered an inferior substitute for MDMA, is in less demand by the abuser population.[51]

Endnotes

1. El Paso Intelligence Center (EPIC), National Seizure System (NSS), methamphetamine laboratory seizure data, run date February 25, 2011.

2. EPIC, NSS, methamphetamine laboratory capacity data for Washington, run date February 25, 2011.

3. Northwest High Intensity Drug Trafficking Area (HIDTA), response to NDIC Request for Information (RFI), April 11, 2011.

4. Northwest HIDTA, *2011 Northwest HIDTA Threat Assessment*, p. 4; Northwest HIDTA, response to NDIC RFI, February 4, 2011.

5. Northwest HIDTA, *2011 Northwest HIDTA Threat Assessment*, p. 4; Northwest HIDTA, response to NDIC RFI, February 4, 2011.

6. Northwest HIDTA, response to NDIC RFI, February 4, 2011.

7. Northwest HIDTA, response to NDIC RFI, March 17, 2011.

8. Northwest HIDTA, response to NDIC RFI, March 17, 2011.

9. Northwest HIDTA, *Northwest HIDTA Newsletter*, January 2011, p. 7.

10. Northwest HIDTA, *Northwest HIDTA Newsletter*, January 2011, p. 7.

11. Northwest HIDTA, *Northwest HIDTA Newsletter*, January 2011, p. 7.

12. Northwest HIDTA, *Northwest HIDTA Newsletter*, January 2011, p. 7.

13. Bureau of Justice Statistics, *Sourcebook of Criminal Justice Statistics Online*, table 4.38.2009, accessed April 18, 2011.

14. Drug Enforcement Administration (DEA), Seattle Field Division, response to NDIC RFI, March 16, 2011.

15. Northwest HIDTA, *2011 Northwest HIDTA Threat Assessment*, p. 17; Northwest HIDTA, response to NDIC RFI, February 4, 2011.

16. Northwest HIDTA, 2011 *Northwest HIDTA Threat Assessment*, p. 17.

17. Northwest HIDTA, response to NDIC RFI, March 29, 2011.

18. Northwest HIDTA, 2010 *Marijuana Eradication Statistics Statewide*, January 4, 2011, p.1; Northwest HIDTA, *Northwest HIDTA Newsletter*, January 2011, p. 8.

19. Kent Justice Training Center, interview with NDIC intelligence analyst (IA), January 25, 2011.

20. Northwest HIDTA, *2011 Northwest HIDTA Threat Assessment*, p. 17.

21. Northwest HIDTA, *2011 Northwest HIDTA Threat Assessment*, p. 17.

22. Northwest HIDTA, response to NDIC RFI, February 4, 2011.

23. Northwest HIDTA, response to NDIC RFI, March 17, 2011.

24. Northwest HIDTA, response to NDIC RFI, March 16, 2011.

25. Northwest HIDTA, response to NDIC RFI, March 16, 2011; Northwest HIDTA, response to NDIC RFI, March 17, 2011.

26. Northwest HIDTA, response to NDIC RFI, March 16, 2011; Northwest HIDTA, response to NDIC RFI, March 17, 2011.

27. Pacific Integrated Border Intelligence Team (IBIT), interview with NDIC IA, January 26, 2011; Northwest HIDTA, response to NDIC RFI, March 31, 2011.

28. Pacific IBIT, interview with NDIC IA, January 26, 2011.

29. Northwest HIDTA, response to NDIC RFI, March 31, 2011.

30. U.S. Customs and Border Protection (CBP), interview with NDIC IA, January 27, 2011; Northwest HIDTA, response to NDIC RFI, March 17, 2011.

31. CBP, interview with NDIC IA, January 27, 2011.

32. Pacific IBIT, interview with NDIC IA, January 26, 2011.

33. CBP, interview with NDIC IA, January 27, 2011.

34. Northwest HIDTA, response to NDIC RFI, May 3, 2011.

35. U.S. Census Bureau, U.S. census population estimates for 2009, accessed April 13, 2010.

36. Canadian Border Patrol, *2 Canadians Arrested in Marijuana Smuggling Case on Olympic Peninsula*, June 1, 2010, p. 1.

37. Northwest HIDTA, *Domestic Highway Enforcement-Northwest HIDTA Threat Assessment 2010*, February 22, 2010, p.1; Northwest HIDTA, *2011 Northwest HIDTA Threat Assessment*, p. 9.

38. Northwest HIDTA, response to NDIC RFI, February 15, 2011.

39. Northwest HIDTA, interview with NDIC IA, February 15, 2011.

40. Northwest HIDTA, *2010 Marijuana Eradication Statistics Statewide*, January 4, 2011, p. 3.

41. Northwest HIDTA, *Northwest HIDTA Newsletter*, January 2011, p. 7; Northwest HIDTA, response to NDIC RFI, May 3, 2011.

42. Northwest HIDTA, *2011 Northwest HIDTA Threat Assessment*, p. 20.

43. Northwest HIDTA, interview with NDIC IA, January 26, 2011; Northwest HIDTA, response to NDIC RFI, April 13, 2011.

44. Northwest HIDTA, interview with NDIC IA, January 26, 2011; Northwest HIDTA, response to NDIC RFI, April 13, 2011.

45. Northwest HIDTA, interview with NDIC IA, January 26, 2011.

46. Northwest HIDTA, response to NDIC RFI, March 31, 2011; Northwest HIDTA, response to NDIC RFI, April 13, 2011.

47. Northwest HIDTA, response to NDIC RFI, May 3, 2011; Northwest HIDTA, *2011 Northwest HIDTA Threat Assessment*, p. 9.

48. Northwest HIDTA, *2011 Northwest HIDTA Threat Assessment*, p. 23.

49. Royal Canadian Mounted Police (RMCP), *RCMP Criminal Intelligence Report on the Illicit Drug Situation in Canada 2009*, accessed April 20, 2011; U.S. Department of Homeland Security, *United States-Canada Joint Border Threat and Risk Assessment*, July 2010, pp. 7–8; DEA, Drug Fact Sheet, *MDMA or Ecstasy*, accessed April 26, 2011; Criminal Intelligence Service Canada, *2009 Report on Organized Crime*, May 2009, p. 31.

50. Northwest HIDTA, *2011 Northwest HIDTA Threat Assessment*, p. 23.

51. Pacific IBIT, interview with NDIC analyst, January 26, 2011.

Sources

Local, State, and Regional

Auburn Police Department
Bellevue Police Department
  Eastside Narcotics Task Force
Bellingham Police Department
Benton County Sheriff's Department
Blaine Police Department
Bonney Lake Police Department
Brier Police Department
Centralia Police Department
Cheney Police Department
Clark County Sheriff's Office
Des Moines Police Department
Edmonds Police Department
  South Snohomish County Narcotics Task Force
Everett Police Department
  Snohomish Regional Drug Task Force
Federal Way Police Department
Ferndale Police Department
Fife Police Department
Kennewick Police Department
Kent Police Department
Kent Regional Justice Center
King County Medical Examiner's Office
King County Sheriff's Office
Kitsap County Sheriff's Office
  West Sound Narcotics Enforcement Team
Lacey Police Department
  Thurston County Narcotics Task Force
Milton Police Department
Mountlake Terrace Police Department
Mukilteo Police Department
Olympia Police Department
  Thurston County Narcotics Task Force
Pierce County Sheriff's Office
Prosser Police Department
Renton Police Department
Richland Police Department
Seattle Police Department
Selah Police Department
Snohomish County Sheriff's Department
  Snohomish Regional Task Force
Snoqualmie Police Department
Spokane County Sheriff's Office
Spokane Police Department
Sultan Police Department
Sumner Police Department

Sunnyside Police Department
Tacoma Police Department
Thurston County Sheriff's Office
Toppenish Police Department
Tukwila Police Department
University of Washington
    Alcohol and Drug Abuse Institute
Vancouver Police Department
Washington State Attorney General's Office
Washington State Department of Social and Health Services
    Division of Alcohol and Substance Abuse
Washington State Patrol
    Investigative Assistance Division
        K-9 Unit, Field Operations Bureau
        Pro-Active Methamphetamine Investigation Team
West Richland Police Department
Yakima Police Department

Federal

Executive Office of the President
    Office of National Drug Control Policy
        High Intensity Drug Trafficking Area
            Northwest
U.S. Department of Agriculture
    U.S. Forest Service
U.S. Department of Health and Human Services
    Substance Abuse and Mental Health Services
    Administration
        Office of Applied Studies
U.S. Department of Homeland Security
    U.S. Coast Guard
    U.S. Customs and Border Protection
    U.S. Immigration and Customs Enforcement
U.S. Department of the Interior
    National Park Service
U.S. Department of Justice
    Bureau of Justice Assistance
        Western States Information Network
    Drug Enforcement Administration
        El Paso Intelligence Center
            National Seizure System
        Federal-Wide Drug Seizure System
        Seattle Division
        System to Retrieve Information From Drug
        Evidence
    Executive Office for U.S. Attorneys
        U.S. Attorneys Offices
            Western District of Washington
    Organized Crime Drug Enforcement Task Force

U.S. Department of Transportation
  Bureau of Transportation Statistics
    Research and Innovative Technology
    Administration
U.S. Department of the Treasury
  Financial Crimes Enforcement Network

Other

National Parks Conservation Association
Pacific Integrated Border Intelligence Team

END